Authentic LEARNING PRACTICE

Delfin Merlan, Ed.D

author HOUSE

AuthorHouse™
1663 Liberty Drive
Bloomington, IN 47403
www.authorhouse.com
Phone: 833-262-8899

Published by AuthorHouse 12/02/2021

ISBN: 978-1-6655-4609-6 (sc)
ISBN: 978-1-6655-4608-9 (e)

Print information available on the last page.

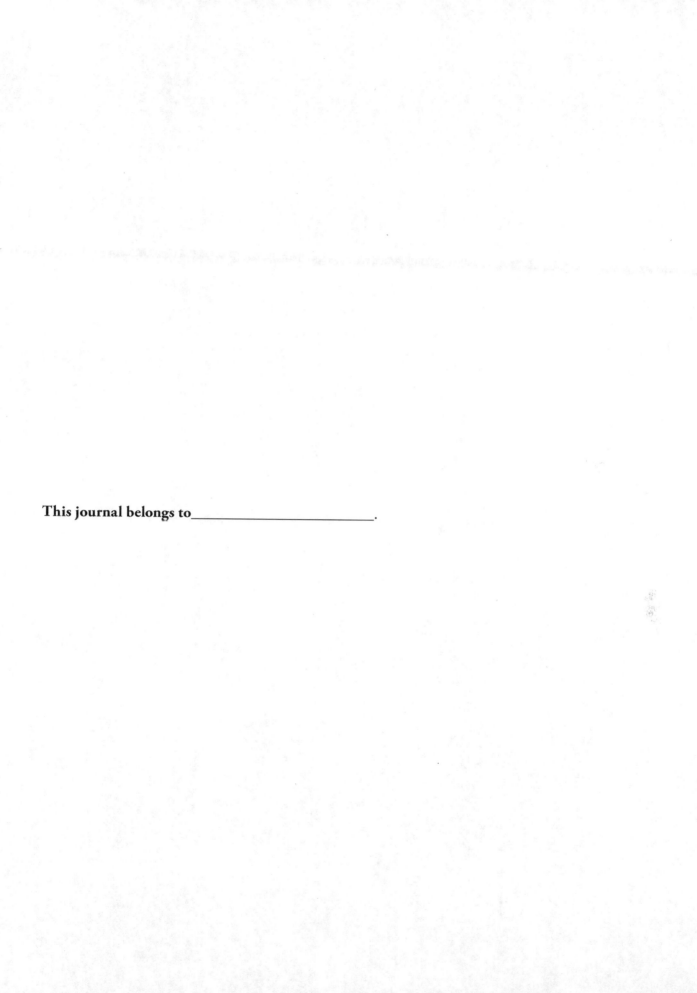

This journal belongs to_____.

Date:

Welcome! This begins the journey towards self-discovery in designing a future filled with abundant possibilities. The possibilities open when a person's beliefs start to match their behavioral practices. This Authentic Learning Experience focuses on your growth and development in attaining your vision.

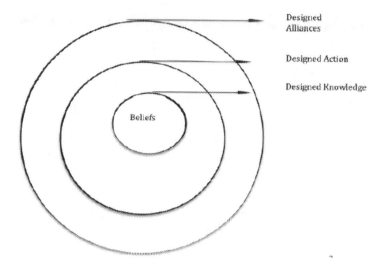

Date:

The Mission is a person's purpose and its reason for existence.
The Vision is the desired future a person envisions.
The Values are the beliefs held.

Identify your Mission, Vision, & Values. What values will you have to attain the Mission & Vision?

Mission

Vision

Values

Delfin Merlan, Ed.D

Designed Knowledge

How is knowledge attained?

Designed Knowledge

Date:

A motto derives from an inspirational quote. A motto we use is a quote from Vince Lombardi. We used his original quote and crafted, "Strength Derived from Unity".

Identify your motivational leadership quotes. Create your own motto.

Motivational Leadership Quotes	My Motto

Delfin Merlan, Ed.D

Designed Knowledge

Date:

Reflect on your beliefs about yourself and how the actions align with one another. What are your beliefs about your future? What are your non-negotiable set of values?

Beliefs	Values

Designed Knowledge

Date:

Imagine 3-5 year goal(s) are created and abundantly attained. What advice or recommendation will you share to a younger you?

Designed Knowledge

Date:

What are your 3-5 year goals and objectives?

Goal #1:

    Objectives

        a.

        b.

        c.

Goal # 2:

    Objectives

        a.

        b.

        c.

Goal # 3:

    Objectives

        a.

        b.

        c.

Delfin Merlan, Ed.D

Designed Knowledge

Date:

How do you shut down distractions in order to hear your inner voice?

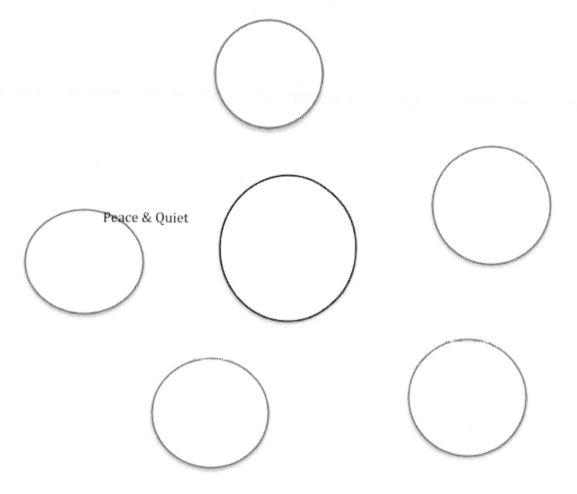

Peace & Quiet

Designed Knowledge

Date:

Create an awareness list of distractions that may take you away from your goals.

1.

2.

3.

4.

5.

6.

7.

8.

9.

10.

Delfin Merlan, Ed.D

Designed Knowledge

Date:

When you find yourself off center or off balance with life, how do you center yourself back to the person who is mindful and aware?

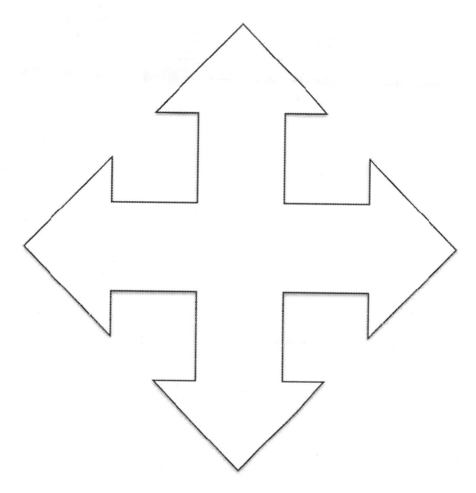

Designed Knowledge

Date:

Our Existence can be described in 3 forms, The Spirit, Body, and Mind. How do you consistently nourish and fill the 3 forms to capacity?

Spirit	Body	Mind

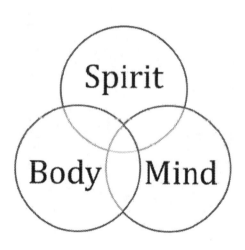

Designed Knowledge

Date:

Using energy in states of being can impede progress that we cannot change; reflect upon experiences, which may keep you in the past state, and design strategies to move you towards the present state and the creative future states.

Staying in the past

Strategies to stay in the present

Strategies to stay in the present Designing the future

Designed Knowledge

Date:

Throughout the day, patterns and behaviors exist to form routines. Change occurs when a pattern of behavior is disrupted. The disruption provides the opportunity to replace existing behaviors, thoughts, and language to form new behaviors. Stay mindful of your day and capture behaviors and patterns you may have from the waking hour to the sleeping hour.

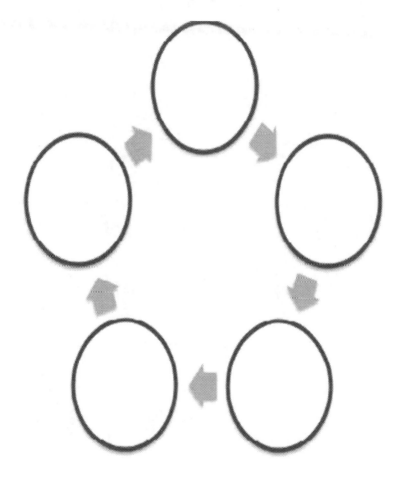

Designed Action

Date:

Routines are embedded when the behaviors become unconscious. From a conscious state, purposefully replace one behavior of the routine with a new practice. Tune in to your feelings and thoughts and observe how others respond to the new practice. Listen to your inner voice throughout the process.

Reflections:

Designed Action

Date:

Observe your colleague(s) and identify patterns and behaviors or routines that may exist throughout their day. Subtly disrupt a routine and pay attention to what occurs when an everyday practice doesn't follow the norm.

Observations:

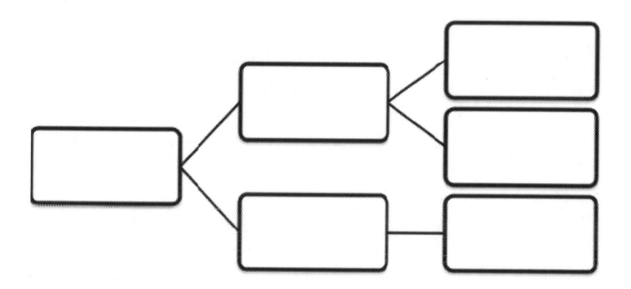

Designed Action

Date:

Design conscious behaviors throughout the day that can provide "a "different outcome". Add new behaviors to shift the pendulum and momentum.

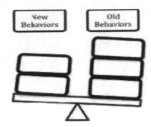

Delfin Merlan, Ed.D

Designed Action

Date:

Perceptions and perspectives play a role in framing our behaviors. Framing is a strategy used to guide behavioral practices. Your beliefs are the center of your frames. Create a sustainable frame for a goal you have identified.

Example: Frame for Growth & Development

Goal: Become Physically Healthy

Patient	Persistent	Dedicated	Eat healthier foods

Beliefs

Participate in physical hobbies that I enjoy   Walk daily   Be outdoors

Designed Knowledge

Date:

Practice reframing language shifting a negative deconstructive frame to a positive constructive frame:

Negative Deconstructive Frame	Positive Constructive Frame
This plan will never work.	
That was the worst idea I have ever heard. We will never finish this project.	
I can't stand this person.	
She has a big mouth. I don't trust her. He's a loser. He is a player.	
I hate this job.	
Our manager doesn't know what he is doing.	
Marijuana is a dangerous drug.	
I would never buy meat. Industries fill the animals with testosterone.	

Delfin Merlan, Ed.D

Designed Action

Date:

Nature provides signs of how growth occurs. Your ideas are seeds. Capture the life cycle of how a seed grows to finally bear fruit. How are ideas similar to the life cycle of a seed? Diagram the life cycle of a seed.

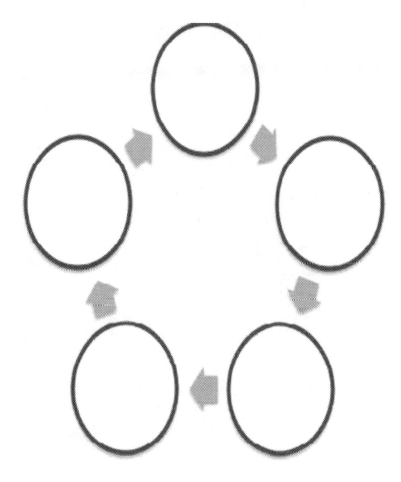

Designed Action

Date:

When a seed is planted, consider the needs to ensure the seed bears fruit. What are nourishments the seed needs? How are the nourishments a metaphor for feeding your seeds of ideas?

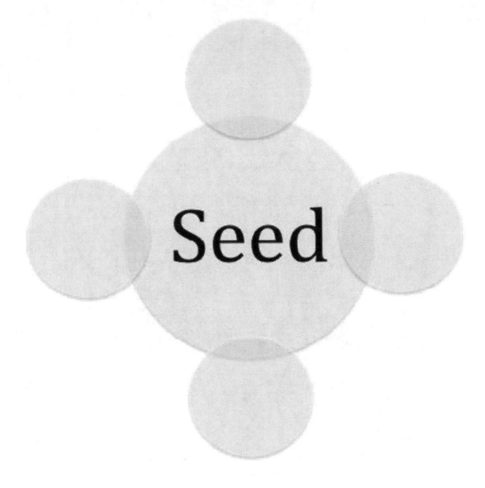

Delfin Merlan, Ed.D

Designed Action

Date:

Reflect back about a high-performing team you were a part of! The team worked well together, everyone made valuable contributions, and work was fun! The team met the goals to everyone's expectations. You enjoyed being on this team.

- What do you remember most about this team?

- What behaviors and/or mindsets did *you* contribute to attain this success?

- How did leadership enable yours and the team's accomplishments?

- What are you hoping in the future with your team?

Designed Alliance

Date:

A random act of kindness has the ability to change the tone and mood of others and set an new trajectory since a new pattern has been established.

Task:

Go to a public place and seek to find an opportunity to perform a random act of kindness in secret. Pay attention to the surroundings and note how you felt when the deed was accomplished. An example may be paying for a family's meal at a restaurant and leaving before anyone can say thank you.

Designed Action

Date:

Distinguishing the difference between a group and a team provides guidelines of how strategize and design outcomes.

Identify a group or groups you are a part of.

1)

2)

3)

4)

5)

Identify a team or teams you are a part of.

1)

2)

3)

4)

5)

Designed Alliances

Date:

Think about a leader, mentor, or role model who was influential in your growth and development as a person. What characteristics did he/she demonstrate that exemplified great leadership?

Identify and briefly describe the characteristics:

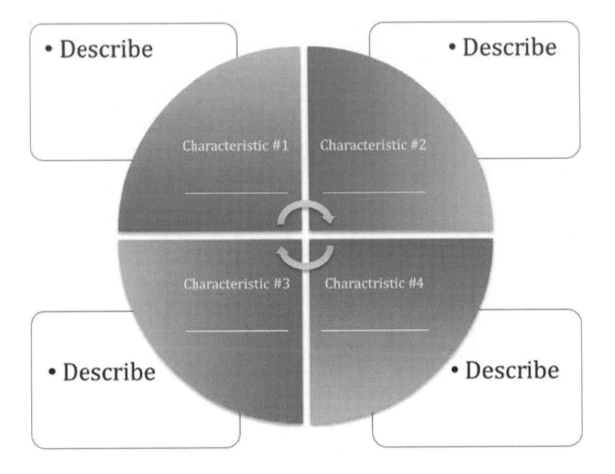

Delfin Merlan, Ed.D

Designed Alliances

Date:

High-performing teams go through stages of development to meet their goal(s). Authentic Learning understands the stages and can bring individuals back to the path towards achievement. The matrix identifies the need to balance relationship and task behaviors by balancing the middle. The leader guides the team through the stages of development.

Authentic Learning Matrix

			Effectiveness
		Collaboration	
	Safety		
Purpose			

Cohesion

Relationship

Behaviors

    Conflict

    Intimacy &
    Inclusion

	Orientation	**Organization**	**Open Data Flow**	**Problem Data**	**Solving Flow**

Task Behaviors

Sharing

Designed Alliances
Date:

Stage 1: Designed Knowledge - Setting the Stage

Purpose

Relationship Behaviors

Intimacy & Inclusion

Orientation
Task Behaviors

Designed Alliances

Date:

Characteristics of Stage 1

Dependency & Orientation - Members are dependent upon the leader for direction. Leader must explain tasks requirements and create commitment to shared goals. The leader creates experiences to form the three following characteristics of Stage 1:

1. *Identity: Who are we? What's our purpose?*

   _____

   _____

   _____

2. *Intimacy: How close will the team work together?*

   _____

   _____

   _____

3. *Inclusion: When an issue arises, how will the team problem solve to form inclusivity?*

   _____

   _____

   _____

Delfin Merlan, Ed.D

Designed Alliances
Date:

These 5 keys of an authentic learning experience can unlock individual and team performance to critically engage its participants and by no means is exhaustive. They establish the promise and power to create a culture of authenticity.

Purpose:
Partnerships:
Safe Practices:
Situational Learning
Shares Responsibilities

Designed Alliances

Date:

Mindful strategies and practices to maximize Return on Efficiency (ROE).

I.	Introduction	VI.	Resources
	a. Leadership		a. Risk
	b. Culture		b. Reward
	c. Need	VII.	Time
II.	Return on Efficiency	VIII.	Appreciation
	a. Sustainability		a. Credibility
	b. Viability		b. Mindset
	c. Soft Skills		c. Framing
III.	Communication	IX.	Connections
	a. Body Language		a. Authentic
	b. Verbal Language		b. Emotional Intelligence
	c. Respect, Mannerisms	X.	Ecosystem
IV.	Pivoting		a. Learning Cycle
	a. Forecasting		b. Benchmark & Milestones
	b. Planning		
	c. Team Development		
V.	Calibrating and Aligning Process Focused Shared Experiences with Energy		
	a. Beliefs		
	b. Values		
	c. Expectations		

Date:

THE FOUR TRUST PRINCIPLES

In order to have shared responsibility and dialogue in a team, there must be trust amongst the members both as a whole and on an intrapersonal level. To create shared responsibility Four Trust Principles to follow are:

1) SHARE OPENLY.

2) "LIVE" THE VALUES.

3) BE CONSISTENT IN YOUR ACTIONS AND BEHAVIORS

4) MODEL AND MIRROR YOUR TEAMATES WORDS AND ACTIONS

Date:

The Four Principles of Trust, serve as the foundation for the next section, *Build Your Box.* Think of a box as something that "holds" your groups trust together. It contains the Four

Principles of Trust, like the four "sides" of your box. It allows group members to share dialogue freely and a space for group members to be open with one another. Within this box you start to develop *Partnerships.* Some things that happen with in this box include:

- Getting to know another as an individual (their hobbies, favorite vacation spot, kid's names, favorite sports teams)
- Understanding peoples hopes and concerns, beliefs, values and strengths
- Having dialogue about the vision, mission and outcomes of the team
- Understanding and defining roles
- Working together to develop how the group will communicate and complete tasks (i.e. is email preferred or meeting face-to-face, where to submit completed assignments/projects, scheduling)
- Determining ways to share information, solve problems, and make decisions

Although these things might seem obvious, often time teams overlook the *process* and jump straight to the *task.* Just ask yourself, "Have I ever worked in isolation and wondered what everyone else is doing?" This is all too common and creates a breakdown in team performance. Remember that in order to avoid such isolation you must communicate openly, you must engage in dialogue.

Delfin Merlan, Ed.D

Date:

Emotional Intelligence

The ability to identify, use, understand, and manage emotions in positive ways. The impact felt helps overcome challenges, defuse conflicts, and manages behaviors for growth to occur. High Emotional Intelligence (EQ) recognizes your own emotional state and states of others, and engages with people in a way that attracts them to you. Understanding Emotional Intelligence helps relate to people, form healthier relationships, and achieves greater success at work, and lead a more fulfilling life. The Four attributes of EQ are as follows:

1) Self-Awareness

2) Self-Management

3) Social Awareness

4) Relationship Management

Raising Emotional Intelligence

Rapidly reduce stress in the moment.

Understand the relationship between stress with emotional awareness.

Matching Verbal & Non-Verbal Communication.

Using humor and play to deal with challenges.

Resolve conflict positively.

Language & Communicating Values

Topic of Inquiry	Traditional Titles
Affirmative Statements	
Valuing Time	
Creating Change Positively	
Respectful Relationships	
Peak Performance	
Positive Cross-Gender Relationships	
Magnetic Customer Experience	
Stories of Passionate Enthusiasm	
Create 2 Topics of Inquiry	

Relationship Behaviors

(Into) Strategy Purpose: Dependency	Appreciative Inquiry, Relationship Development Dependency – The leader must explain the task requirement and generate a common commitment to the shared goals.

Delfin Merlan, Ed.D

(Through) Application	Guiding Questions
Activity, Deliverable, Handout	
(Beyond) Next Steps	Assessing knowledge, intimacy and inclusion.
Where do I go from here? What do I do with this information now?	*Resource: Appreciative Inquiry: Change at the Speed of Imagination by Jane Watkins, Bernard Mohr, and Ralph Kelly (2011)*

Task Behaviors

(Into) Strategy	Appreciative Inquiry
Purpose: Orientation	**Orientation**- What is required of me? Purpose, Common Goals, Individual strengths. What are the expectations of each member with regard to quality, timelines, addressing issues, etc.
(Through) Application	Norm Setting
Activity, Deliverable, Handout	

(Beyond) Next Steps Where do I go from here? What do I do with this information now?	Develop Identity Established agreed upon norms, beliefs, values, and expectations. Develop poster for all to see. Monitor and balance task and relationship behaviors. Resource: *Great Meetings Great Results by Dee Kelsey and Pam Plumb (2004)*

Task Activity: Norm Setting, Self-Assessment Role Questionnaire/Exploration

After completing this activity, create "paired groups" based on strengths/weaknesses.)

Purpose of the Team: Goals of the Team: My Role on this team is: My Strengths are: Reasons: My Weaknesses are:	
Reasons:	
The role of my teammates is: Team member #1 Team member #2 Team member #3 Team member #4 Team member #5	

Delfin Merlan, Ed.D

Task Activity: Quick Steps in Norm-Setting: Established Groups

Distribute 3x5 Cards to each committee member

Ask them to write one norm or expectation they have to make the meetings run smoothly. Have a recorder write comments on a large piece of whiteboard that all can see. Go around the table and let each person state one norm from a card (i.e. begin and end on time).

After each member's statement, ask the group if they agree or have some reservations about that norm.

When the group reaches consensus about the norm, leave it on the whiteboard. Move to the next person and repeat steps 4 and 5.

Continue until all cards have been read and norms established. This process should not take longer than 15 minutes.

Post the norms at every meeting of the group.

Plan of Action & Milestones

Task	Due Date	Deliverable	Responsibility	Notes

Finishing Strong: Wrapping-Up

Task:

- ✓ Summary of the Norms of the Team
- ✓ Identify Roles of the Team
- ✓ Identify Purpose of the Team
- ✓ Identify expected timeline

Clarification:

- ✓ Seek any clarification questions
- ✓ Exchange contact information
- ✓ Determine best way of communication

Relationship:

- ✓ End on a positive note
- ✓ A thank you message
- ✓ Communicate appreciation for the work about to be done
- ✓ Raffle
- ✓ Something fun and engaging for the newly formed team

Self-Assessment Rating

1:Needs More Work   **2:Communicated**   **3: Buy-In**   **4:Great Start**

Stage 1	1	2	3	4	Notes
Time was spent developing the relationship of the group.					

Delfin Merlan, Ed.D

Time was spent getting to know the individual strengths of the team.					
The purpose was clearly identified and easily understood by all members on the team.					
The goals of the team were clearly communicated.					
The members of the team understand their role(s).					
The team norms were developed. Each member on the team understands how we will work and treat each other if an issue arises.					
This meeting was a good beginning					
The team members rated this meeting a					
My Overall Rating					

Stage 2: Designed Action - Developing a Safe Environment

Safety

Relationship Behaviors

Conflict

Organization

Task Behaviors

Introduction

Characteristics of Stage 2

Safety – When members of the team feel safe, they are empowered to act, take risks, and asks questions to respectfully challenge their colleagues. Leader must create the culture and skill set by modeling desired behaviors of the group

4. Fractionation:

_____

_____

_____

5. Reactive:

_____

_____

_____

6. Disagreements:

_____

_____

_____

Communication

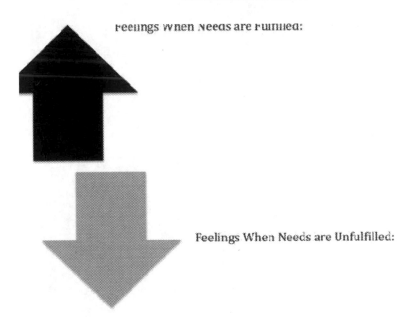

Feelings When Needs are Fulfilled:

Feelings When Needs are Unfulfilled:

Delfin Merlan, Ed.D

Understanding Conflict

Conflict: _____

_____

_____

_____

Sources of Conflict	
1. Resources	
2. Styles	
3. Perceptions	
4. Goals	
4. Goals	
5. Pressures	
6. Roles	
7. Personal Values	
8. Unpredictable Policies	

Performance

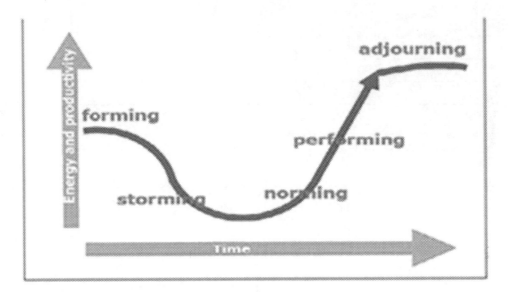

Physiological Response:

_____

_____

_____

_____

Staying Mindful & Pro-Active:

_____

_____

_____

_____

Tips for resolving conflict in a trust-building way:

- **Stay focused in the present.** When you are not holding on to old hurts and resentments, you can recognize the reality of a current situation and view it as a new opportunity for resolving old feelings about conflicts.

- **Choose your arguments.** Arguments take time and energy, especially if you want to resolve them in a positive way. Consider what is worth arguing about and what is not.

- **Forgive.** Other people's hurtful behavior is in the past. To resolve conflict, you need to give up the urge to punish or seek revenge.

End conflicts that can't be resolved. It takes two people to keep an argument going. You can choose to disengage from a conflict, even if you still disagree.

Relationship Behavior

(Into) Strategy Purpose: Conflict	Coaching/Mentoring Conflict: Teams go through a period of internal strife, most often centered on the struggle for leadership or influence within the group. Unless the group faces this conflict, it will not progress to the next stage and become stagnant.
(Through) Application Activity, Deliverable, Handout	Values Co-Active Coaching Designed Alliance
(Beyond) Next Steps	Assessing and managing conflict
Where do I go from here? What do I do with this information now?	*Resource: Co-Active Coaching: New Skills for Coaching People Towards Success in Work and Life by Laura Whitworth, Karen Kimsey-House etc. (2009)*

Relationship Activity: Values Work Sheet

This exercise is designed to assist the team in identifying their values.

Prioritize and List Values	Value/Description	Score Level of Satisfaction Scale of 1-10 (10 being the highest)

Relationship Activity: Designed Alliance

Powerful Questions are thought-provoking queries that bring clarity to an issue. By asking the powerful question, the coach invites clarity, action, and discovery with the possibility for expanded learning and a fresh perspective.

Coaches and _____ begin designing their _____ during the _____ session. Both client and coach are intimately involved in _____ the _____ _____ that will be the most beneficial to the_____.

Designed alliances tend to shift over time and need to be _____ regularly.

Starting a Coaching Session	Assignment
What's occurred since we last spoke? What would you like to talk about? What's new? How was your week? How is the team progressing?	1. Create 5 powerful questions designed at getting to know what a person values. 2. Practice Co-Active Coaching with a partner.

Question Topic Examples

Assessment	Goals	Implementation
What do you think is best?	What do you want?	What is the action plan?
How does it look to you?	What are your desired outcomes?	What steps are required of us?
How do you feel about it?	What are the needs?	What support is needed to accomplish our task?
What resonates with you?	How attainable are the goals?	What is your role?
Rate the issue from 1-5.	What steps will have to occur?	How will the team understand their role?
What are your thoughts?	When you are successful how will you know?	What is the desired timeline to meet our goals?

Task Behavior

(Into) Strategy	Coaching
Purpose: Conflict	Organization – The group arrives to common understanding of the task's requirement, and can organize itself to achieve its goals. Unless the goals are clear, the group will flow between Stage 1 and Stage 2.

(Through) Application Activity, Deliverable, Handout	Non-Violent Communication Confrontational Coaching
(Beyond) Next Steps Where do I go from here? What do I do with this information now?	Assessing and managing conflict *Resource: The Eight Essential Steps to Conflict Resolution: Preserving Relationships at Work, at Home, and the Community by Dudle Weeks, Ph.D (1994)*

A Four-Part Process

<u>Observation</u>

I	You

<u>Feelings</u>

I	You

<u>Needs</u>

I	You

<u>Requests</u>

I	You

Delfin Merlan, Ed.D

Clarifying Perceptions of the Conflict

Here are important questions to ask when gaining perspective of the conflict:

1. Conflict is over one isolated event with little consistency with the rest of the relationship, or the latest of a series of conflicts revealing problems within the relationship as a whole, How does the leader bring clarity to the issue?
2. The conflict is with the other party and not a conflict within myself?
3. What is the conflict about? What is it not about?
4. Is the conflict is over values or preferences?
5. Is the conflict over needs or desires?
6. Is the conflict over goals or methods?
7. What are the elements of the conflict?
8. Which do I feel most strongly about?
9. Which should I deal with first? Which will be addressed most effectively?

Action Learning Cycles

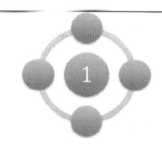

Finishing Strong: Wrapping-Up

Task:

✓ Reinforce the norms developed by the group

✓ Develop questions to clarify conflict

✓ Understand the stage of the process

✓ Practice being mindful and aware

Clarification:

✓ Seek any clarification on issues

✓ Use questions to address issues

✓ Gauge the members of the team

✓ Body matches verbal language

Relationship:

✓ End on a positive note

✓ Issues are brought up respectfully

✓ All Input is considered

✓ Communicate the mission, goals, norms &

✓ values of the team

✓ Walk the talk

Self-Assessment Rating

1:Needs More Work   **2:Communicated**   **3: Buy-In**   **4:Great Start**

Stage 2	1	2	3	4	Notes
Safety is exhibited through psychological, physical, social, and emotional practices.					
I understand how do manage conflict and the sources of conflict.					
Positive feedback utilizes Co-Active Coaching to develop an individuals emotional strength.					

Delfin Merlan, Ed.D

Corrective feedback is used in a respectful and instructive manner so participants are encouraged and motivated to act.					
A socially responsible environment where participants are encouraged to take risks and learn from trial and error is formed due to modeling and feedback provided.					
Leaders foster strong (psychological, physical, social, and emotional) team bonds for high-performance to occur by developing situational learning for teams to participate in.					
Leaders create fun and motivating learning environments to reduce stress by having a clear perspective.					
Leaders are perceived as caring, supportive, and motivational leaders concerned for the safety and well-being of the team and individuals.					
The team members rated this meeting a					
My Overall Rating					

Summary

Date:

Stage 3: Designed Alliance - Building Shared Responsibility

Collaboration

Relationship Behaviors
Cohesion

Open Data Flow
Task Behaviors

Introduction

Delfin Merlan, Ed.D

Characteristics of Stage 3

Situational Learning and Partnerships: Team Members start to share information and work within the team structures. The leader monitors and assesses teamwork by placing the groups in Situational Learning Activities for partnerships to develop. Leader must explain tasks requirements and create opportunities for team members to work together.

7. Sharing:

_____

_____

_____

8. Dialogue:

_____

_____

_____

9. Trust:

_____

_____

Enabling Action with Questions

Questions raise awareness; they ask participants what they think and feel about something.

The What?

What reaction did you have when hearing this lesson?

What happened there?

What jumped out at you when you saw this for the first time?

What were your feelings? About the presentation

What stood out for you?

What did you hear that you don't already know?

So What?

What is your perspective regarding the main points of view in this presentation?

What can be expected from the team?

What ideas do you have?

What concerns does this raise for you?

What has been done about these problems so far?

What outcome would you like to see?

Now What?

What will you do differently?

What are the implications if nothing is done? What will you do first to get started?

What possibilities exist that weren't obvious before?

What learning's are you taking forward out of this experience?

Relationship Behavior

(Into) Strategy Purpose: Cohesion	Social Learning Theory Cohesion: Feelings of relief and increased trust in each other brings a sense of "we're all in this together." This is not the optimal phase, however, the team members feel better.
(Through) Application Activity, Deliverable, Handout	Collaborative Team Presentation Developing Questions Project Based Learning/Competition
(Beyond) Next Steps	Providing Feedback and Coaching
Where do I go from here? What do I do with this information now?	Making Questions Work: A Guide to What and How Facilitators, Consultants, Managers, Coaches, and Educators by Dorothy Strachan (2007)

Strength Assessment

Prior to the Team Meeting each person on the team takes an assessment to determine his/her leadership style. Spend a few minutes writing the answers to these questions prior to going into groups.

Delfin Merlan, Ed.D

Answer the following questions as a group.

<table>
<tr><td colspan="1">

Overview Question:

What are the benefits of using a perspective that emphasizes strengths as opposed to weaknesses in a team environment?
</td></tr>
<tr><td>

Whole Group Dialogue & Conversation

   1. Discuss with the group the strength(s) that you work out of most often?

   2. Discuss how they can be misperceived.

   3. Key Findings

Other
</td></tr>
</table>

"What we focus on changes the biological structure of our brains
and creates a biological self-fulfilling prophecy."

<table>
<tr><td>

Questions Regarding Team Insight & Experience
</td></tr>
<tr><td>

Form small groups based on strengths.

   1. Describe the role you usually play on a team.

   2. How does that relate to your strengths?

   3. What is the best experience you have had on a team?

   4. What is the worse experience you have had on a team?

   5. Of all the teams you have been on, you chose those two teams. Why do they hold your attention?

   6. Does your history with teams affect the way you behave in teams currently?

Other

Notes:
</td></tr>
</table>

Developing Awareness through Questions

Form small groups based on strengths.
    1. How can we develop strategies to avoid these situations?
 	
    2. How can a strengths approach help with "other awareness"?
 	
Directions: Develop three questions to develop awareness of the team dynamics.
    3.
 	
    4.
 	
    5.
 	
Notes:

Developing Strengths through Change

Form small groups based on strengths.
    1. Get with a person that shares a similar strength and discuss how people with your strength respond to change.
 	
    2. Is there a difference if the change is imposed or self-initiated?
 	
Directions: Develop three questions to develop awareness of change.
    3.
 	
    4.
 	
    5.
 	
Notes:

Different Drivers of Trust

Provide and example of the following terms in action: Respect

Understanding

Congruency

Communication

Forgiveness

Team Building and Trust

Whole Group Dialogue & Conversation

1. How does knowing your team's strengths affect the level of trust?

2. Can you see how strengths relate to these drivers?

Directions: Develop three questions as a team to develop awareness of change.

3.

4.

5.

Notes:

Self-Management

Form Small Groups based on strengths.

1. Find someone that has at least one strength the same as you.

2. What can be the shadow side of this strength?

3. How do you manage this strength?

4.

5.

6.

Other:

Notes:

Relationship Activity: Team Presentation

The content can be determined based on the leader. The key is to understand the team dynamics operating within this stage. This assignment will challenge the group to reinforce the learning from the previous two stages.

General Guidelines for Presenting as a Team.

Practice the presentation together as a team.

_____

_____

_____

Introduce yourself and the members of the team.

_____

_____

_____

Use the introduction to preview the content of the presentation and how the team will present it. Plan clear transitions between speaker segments.

_____

_____

_____

Determine Visual aids used in the presentation, should all follow the same format.

_____

_____

_____

All team members should be available for the Question and Answer session at the end of the presentation

_____

_____

_____

Q&A.

_____

_____

_____

Delfin Merlan, Ed.D

Team Projects - Oral Presentation Rubric (Use to Score Other Teams)

CATEGORY	4	3	2	1
Preparedness	The team is completely prepared and has obviously rehearsed.	The team seems pretty prepared but might have needed a couple more rehearsals.	The team is somewhat prepared, but it is clear that rehearsal was lacking.	The team does not seem at all prepared to present.
Enthusiasm	Facial expressions and body language generate a strong interest and enthusiasm about the topic in others.	Facial expressions and body language sometimes generate a strong interest and enthusiasm about the topic in others.	Facial expressions and body language are used to try to generate enthusiasm, but seem somewhat faked.	Very little use of facial expressions or body language. Did not generate much interest in topic being presented.
Speaks Clearly	Speaks clearly and distinctly all (100-95%) the time, and mispronounces no words.	Speaks clearly and distinctly all (100-95%) the time, but mispronounces one word.	Speaks clearly and distinctly most (94-85%) of the time. Mispronounces no more than one word.	Often mumbles or cannot be understood OR mispronounces more than one word.
Props/Visuals	Student uses prop/visuals that shows considerable work/creativity and which makes the presentation better.	Student uses prop/visuals that shows some work/creativity and which makes the presentation better.	Student uses prop/visual that makes the presentation better.	Student uses no props/visuals OR the prop/visuals chosen detracts from the presentation.
Stays on Topic	Stays on topic all (100%) of the time.	Stays on topic most (99-90%) of the time.	Stays on topic some (89-75%) of the time.	It was hard to tell what the topic was.
Content	Shows a good understanding of the topic.	Shows a good understanding of most of the topic.	Shows a good understanding of parts of the topic.	Does not seem to understand the topic very well.
Presentation on the Whole	Overall, the presentation was excellent.	Overall, the presentation was well done.	Overall, the presentation was average.	Overall, the presentation was poor.

Peer Collaboration and Teamwork

Criteria	Weight	Unsatisfactory	Proficient	Advanced
Leadership and Initiative	25%	Group member played a passive role, generating few new ideas; tended to do only what they were told to do by others or did not seek help when needed.	Group members played an active role in generating new ideas, took initiative in getting tasks organized and completed, and sought help when needed.	*In addition to Proficient criteria:* The group member provided leadership to the group by thoughtfully organizing and dividing the work, checking on progress, or providing focus and direction for the project.
Facilitation and Support	25%	Group member seemed unable or unwilling to help others, made non-constructive criticisms toward the project or other group members, or distracted other members.	Group members demonstrated willingness to help other group members when asked, actively listened to the ideas of others, and helped create a positive work environment.	*In addition to Proficient criteria:* The group member actively checked with others to understand how each member was progressing and how he or she may be of help.
Contributions and Work Ethic	50%	Group member was often off-task, did not complete assignments or duties, or had attendance problems that significantly impeded progress on project. May have worked hard, but on relatively unimportant parts of the project.	Group member was prepared to work each day, met due dates by completing assignments/duties, and worked hard on the project most of the time. If absent, other group members knew the reason and progress was not significantly impeded.	*In addition to Proficient criteria:* The group member made up for work left undone by other group members and demonstrates willingness to spend significant time outside of class/school to complete the project.

Team Presentation: Guide to Help you Plan Your Class Presentation				
CATEGORY	4	3	2	1
Preparedness	Student is completely prepared and has obviously rehearsed.	Student seems pretty prepared but might have needed a couple more rehearsals.	The student is somewhat prepared, but it is clear that rehearsal was lacking.	Student does not seem at all prepared to present.
Comprehension	Student is able to accurately answer almost all questions posed by classmates about the topic.	Student is able to accurately answer most questions posed by classmates about the topic.	Student is able to accurately answer a few questions posed by classmates about the topic.	Student is unable to accurately answer questions posed by classmates about the topic.
Content	Shows a full understanding of the topic.	Shows a good understanding of the topic.	Shows a good understanding of parts of the topic.	Does not seem to understand the topic very well.
Posture and Eye Contact	Stands up straight, looks relaxed and confident. Establishes eye contact with everyone in the room during the presentation.	Stands up straight and establishes eye contact with everyone in the room during the presentation.	Sometimes stands up straight and establish eye contact.	Slouches and/or does not look at people during the presentation.
Collaboration with Peers	Almost always listens to, shares with, and supports the efforts of others in the group. Tries to keep people working well together.	Usually listens to, shares with, and supports the efforts of others in the group. Does not cause "waves" in the group.	Often listens to, shares with, and supports the efforts of others in the group but sometimes is not a good team member.	Rarely listens to, shares with, and supports the efforts of others in the group. Often is not a good team member.

Volume	Volume is loud enough to be heard by all audience members throughout the presentation.	Volume is loud enough to be heard by all audience members at least 90% of the time.	Volume is loud enough to be heard by all audience members at least 80% of the time.	Volume often too soft to be heard by all audience members.
Stays on Topic	Stays on topic all (100%) of the time.	Stays on topic most (99-90%) of the time.	Stays on topic some (89%-75%) of the time.	It was hard to tell what the topic was.

Task Behavior

(Into) Strategy Purpose: Cohesion	Social Learning Theory Open Data Flow – It is time to ensure that all available data within the group that are relevant to the task be available to all members. This means sharing facts, opinions, feelings, hunches, connections, networks, etc. etc., with everyone.
(Through) Application Activity, Deliverable, Handout	Competitive Team Games Project Based Learning/Competition
(Beyond) Next Steps Where do I go from here? What do I do with this information now?	Providing Feedback and Coaching

Task Activity: Tennis Basketball

Object: The first team to put all the tennis balls into the basket wins. Materials: 20-25 Tennis Balls, Basket

Directions:

1) Divide up the teams evenly.

2) Give each team 5 tennis balls.

Delfin Merlan, Ed.D

3) The team will have 3-5 minutes to plan the order and strategy for the game.

4) The tennis ball is passed from one person to another. A successful pass entails the ball bouncing one time to a team member with the receiver successfully catching the ball.

5) Only one tennis ball may be passed at one time.

6) The team will determine their shooter. After each person has successfully caught the ball the shooter may take a shot.

7) When the shooter makes a basket another tennis ball starts through the team.

8) When a ball is dropped or a basket is missed the team must to start all over with

9) the ball in play.

10) The winning team will be the first team to put all 5 tennis balls into the basket.

11) Challenge: During the second round take away verbal communication during the game.

12) Use smaller bouncy balls or various types of balls.

Lessons Learned Recap

What did you like about this activity?

Tell us about the strategy your team used for the game?

What made your team successful?

What obstacles did you have to overcome?

How does this activity relate to your team you work with?

What lessons can you pass along that you learned from this activity?

Task Activity: Structure Build

Object: Build a bridge structure with the ability to hold up a water bottle for one minute. Materials: Several Stacks of newspaper, masking tape, and a water bottle

Directions:
1) Divide up the teams evenly.

2) Give each team a stack of newspaper and some tape. Preferably masking tape.

3) The team will have 5 minutes to plan their strategy to build a structure. When the teams start building the structure no verbal communication is allowed.

4) Allow 5 minutes for the build.

5) After 5 minutes allow the team to plan discuss their strategy for 4 minutes.

6) The team will be given 4 minutes to build their structure.

7) The team will be given 3 minutes to plan and discuss their strategy.

8) The team will be given 3 minutes to build their structure.

9) Repeat until you reach one minute.

10) The winning team will have built the structure that will be able to hold the water bottle for one minute.

At the end of the build, have each team walk around each group and place the water bottle of top of their structure. The structure with the ability to hold up the water bottle wins the game.

Lessons Learned Recap

What did you like about this activity?

Tell us about the strategy your team used for the game?

What made your team successful?

What obstacles did you have to overcome?

Delfin Merlan, Ed.D

How does this activity relate to your team you work with?

What lessons can you pass along that you learned from this activity?

Finishing Strong: Wrapping-Up

Task:

- ✓ Ensure knowledge and information is shared
- ✓ Develop questions to drive action
- ✓ Understand the stage of the process
- ✓ Monitor teams and progress
- ✓ Create project-based learning teams
- ✓ Identify team leader(s)

Clarification:

- ✓ Seek any clarification on issues
- ✓ Provide resources if necessary
- ✓ Provide guidelines and questions for teams
- ✓ Body matches verbal language
- ✓ Relationship:
- ✓ End on a positive note
- ✓ Thank the team for their work
- ✓ Show appreciation
- ✓ Develop leadership within the team
- ✓ Walk the talk

Self-Assessment Rating

1:Needs More Work	2:Communicated		3: Buy-In	4:Great Start	

Stage 3	1	2	3	4	Notes
A positive learning culture is formed as the leader uses games, trial and error, and experiential learning providing new opportunities for participants to engage and try.					
The leader communicates the evaluation process to motivate participants.					
Strength based approaches are used to foster growth and development.					
Knowledge is facilitated throughout the organization rather than seen as the experts of knowledge.					
Participants engage in the material and have time to process the information.					
Participants are building internal representation of the knowledge and interpretation of personal experience gained. Leaders engineer situations for individuals and teams to problem solve by providing an atmosphere of trial and error through practice. Members learn to deal with conflict, engage in problem solving, and seek positive solutions. By nurturing leadership potential, through social-constructivist practices, high-performing teams are formed due to participants critically engaging in the subject.					
Participants are assigned new problems, situations, and experiences to problem solve and learn.					

Delfin Merlan, Ed.D

Relationships are formed to foster motivation so feedback can be provided.					
The leader communicates the evaluation process to motivate participants.					
Participants are encouraged to have fun learning, and motivated improve and share knowledge with their peers.					
Mistakes are seen as opportunities for learning.					

Summary

Stage 4: Strengthening Designed Alliance - High-Performance

Effectiveness

Relationship Behaviors

Cohesion

Problem Solving
Task Behaviors

Introduction

Delfin Merlan, Ed.D

Characteristics of Stage 4

The foundation has been established for teams to work interdependently of the leader. The team has the skills, strategies, and resources to succeed. The leaders role and responsibility shifts to delegating responsibility or empowering others to act. The leader monitors progress and stays pro-active checking in with the teams.

Interdependence

_____

_____

_____

Problem-Solving

_____

_____

_____

Collaboration

_____

_____

_____

Synergy

_____

_____

_____

Characteristics in Action

Integrity	Authenticity	Mutual Respect
Maintain Objectivity Clarify confidentiality Be sensitive to conflicts of interest Avoid Collusion Ask questions fairly Determine authorship Address imbalances in power and information Identify 3 other actions describing integrity: 1. 2. 3.	Build group ownership for outcomes Minimize self-deception Be clear about intentions Acknowledge problems Be honest Be present, tune in Hear various perspectives Identify 3 other actions describing integrity: 1. 2. 3.	Enable equity Clarify group norms Respect exchange times Encourage direct interaction Be patient; whose silence is it? Respect the energy of the group. Identify 3 other actions describing mutual respect: 1. 2. 3.

Practicing Integrity

Integrity	Stop Doing	Start Doing	Continue Doing
Maintain Objectivity Clarify confidentiality Be sensitive to conflicts of interest Avoid Collusion			

Delfin Merlan, Ed.D

Ask questions fairly			
Determine authorship Address imbalances in power and information Other			

Practicing Authenticity

Authenticity	Stop Doing	Start Doing	Continue Doing
Build group ownership for outcomes Minimize self-deception Be clear about intentions Acknowledge problems Be honest Be present, tune in Hear various perspectives Other			

Practicing Mutual Respect

Integrity	Stop Doing	Start Doing	Continue Doing
Enable equity			
Clarify group norms			
Respect exchange times			
Encourage direct interaction			
Be patient; whose silence is it?			
Respect the energy of the group.			
Other			

Process Framework: Process & Content Neutrality

Three perspectives are always in consideration from the broader context; the individual, the team, and the organization. Although, these areas can be thought of sequentially in how progression flows, in practice, they can emerge in various ways at different times.

Determine questions and follow-up questions from listening to what participants say.

1. Making assumptions and perspectives explicit.
2. Understanding interests and power relationships.
3. Exploring alternative ways of thinking and acting.
4. Making ethical choices.

Delfin Merlan, Ed.D

Modeling the Process Framework for Addressing Issues

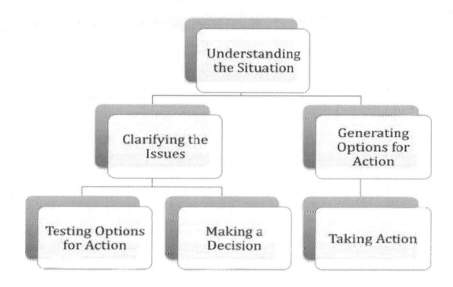

Notes: _____

_____

_____

_____

_____

Looking Backward

Key process steps to consider when looking backwards into the development process.

1. Management of the Process
2. Midway through the process
3. The experience as a whole
4. Learning
5. Productivity

Reflection:

What was your overall experience learning about the process of developing high-performing teams?

Question Bank: Looking Backward Examples

- On a scale from 1-4 where 4 is excellent, how would you describe the process you went through?

- What specific times of the event were you aware of having heightened emotions?

- If you could change anything about the sessions, what would it be?

- If there were one thing that stood out for you during our learning, what would it be?

- Did your thoughts help or hinder your participation?

- What did you like most about our meeting?

- What three things will you take back to your team that made the most impact for you?

- What can be improved so we can meet our goals? Develop three more questions to look backward and reflect?

<table>
<tr><td></td></tr>
<tr><td></td></tr>
<tr><td></td></tr>
</table>

Question Bank: Moving Forward Examples

Key process steps to consider when moving forward into the development process.

Celebrating Success

Building ownership for follow-through

Taking action-knowledge transition

Future Collaboration

Reflection:

Moving forward what suggestions do you have about this process?

Question Bank: Moving Forward Examples

- What are your thoughts moving forward:

- What are your thoughts moving forward?

- What possible issues, if any do you see emerging?

- What three things will you take with you after our time together?

- When resolving conflict, what reminders will you have to keep you pro-active?

- What are the first words that come to mind to describe how you feel moving forward?

- Should we be accountable to one another in any way throughout the year? If yes, why? If no, why not?

- If you were uncomfortable with some aspect of the process just completed, how could we address that before moving forward?

Develop three more questions to moving forward?

| |
| |
| |

Finishing Strong: Wrapping-Up

Task:

- ✓ Reinforce the norms developed by the group
- ✓ Develop questions to clarify conflict
- ✓ Understand the stage of the process
- ✓ Practice being mindful and aware

Clarification:

- ✓ Seek any clarification on issues
- ✓ Use questions to address issues
- ✓ Gauge the members of the team
- ✓ Body matches verbal language

Relationship:

- ✓ End on a positive note
- ✓ Issues are brought up respectfully
- ✓ All Input is considered
- ✓ Communicate the mission, goals, norms & values of the team
- ✓ Walk the talk

Delfin Merlan, Ed.D

Self-Assessment Rating

1:Needs More Work	2:Communicated	3: Buy-In	4:Great Start

Stage 4	1	2	3	4	Notes
Clear guidelines are provided for participants to follow					
Communication is effective					
The use of leaders can be seen to lead project teams					
Leaders reflect on personal assumptions, transfer insight and knowledge, engage in the process of problem solving, and they collaboratively work to solve problems					
Participants learn to develop, practice, monitor, and attain goals					
Tools and resources are provided to develop future leaders, and to enhance leadership skills. The leader engages in mentoring others					
Leaders mentor and check progress of goals					
Leader challenge old assumptions by modeling and questioning outdated practices					
Action learning cycles are formed to check for progress and improvement					

A learning culture is formed and promotes and delegates responsibilities to strengthen individuals, teams, and subsequently the organization					
Teamwork and interdependence are seen as individuals work collaboratively to reach individual and team goals					
The team members rated this meeting a					
My Overall Rating					

Date:

Guiding Questions to reflect upon:

How does a leader attain power?

How does a leader influence attitudes?

How does a leader know when followers are engaged and ready for change?

Date:

Practice inquiry when working with others. Here are some guiding questions. Pay attention to the person's body language, tone, and energy through your senses. Pick up on the cues and subtleties in the conversation.

Assessment	Goals	Implementation
What do you think is best?	What do you want?	What is the action plan?
How does it look to you?	What are your desired outcomes?	What steps are required of us?
How do you feel about it?	What are the needs?	What support is needed to accomplish our task?
What resonates with you?	How attainable are the goals?	What is your role?
Rate the issue from 1-5.	What steps will have to occur?	How will the team understand their role?
What are your thoughts?	When you are successful how will you know?	What is the desired timeline to meet our goals?

Delfin Merlan, Ed.D

Date:

Staying mindful and pro-active

Throughout coaching and mentoring, the natural process of a sharing will go through ebbs and flows in the relationship. The dynamic process takes shape by observing and reflecting on the conversation after the meeting. The ability to listen with empathy and compassion guides next steps in forming an alliance to work together.

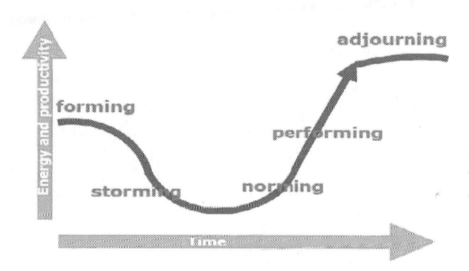

Conflict Resolution

Counter Culture

Eyes of Nature

Sustainability

Energy of Play

Printed in the United States
by Baker & Taylor Publisher Services